TEACHING KIDS ABOUT APOSTROPHE "S" IN POSSESSIVES

David's 23rd Psalm

Habakkuk Educational Materials

Published by Habakkuk Educational Materials

Copyright © 2019-2022 Habakkuk Educational Materials. All rights reserved.

TEACHING KIDS ABOUT APOSTROPHE "S" IN POSSESSIVES

Copyright © 2019-2022 by Habakkuk Educational Materials

No part of this book without a reproducible notice affixed to the footnote may be reproduced in any form or by any electronic or mechanical means, including information storage and retrieval systems, without the written consent of the publisher. If a page is specified as reproducible, the reproduction is permitted for non-commercial, classroom use only. Please address your inquiries to Habakkuk@cox.net.

ISBN (Hardback Edition): 978-1-954796-51-5
ISBN (Paperback Edition): 978-1-954796-07-2

Illustrations: Certain copyrighted images in the interior of this book are used under license from stock.adobe.com. These include the *farmers' chores* image (farmers) by annagarmatiy and (tractor) by naulicreative; the *Aaron's bowl* image by Jakkarin 14; the *Alexander's bread* image by Tigatelu; the *April's comprehension* image by Kankhem; the *Jupiter's glow* image by Assumon; the *Asia's education* image by PikePicture; the *Jesse's paper* image by sabelskaya; the *Benjamin's effort* image by Yusufdemirci; the *Caleb's email* image by Ann131313.A; the *Carole's advice* image by PikePicture; the *David's 23rd Psalm* image by Yoeyoed413; the *Adam's paradise* image by Daria; the *Egypt's future* image by Klyaksun; the *Abraham's beloved children* image by nadia_snopek; the *Elijah's guest* image by Tigatelu; the *Christian's gear* image by Vectorkif; the *Elisha's guidance* image by Inspiring.Team; the Rhoda image by Nizova Tina; the *Rachel's loaves* image by Good Studio; the *Haven's height*, *Isaac's juice*, and *Josiah's salt* images by Yusufdemirci; the Jason image by Toyotoyo; the Oklahoma image by dusica69; the *Jerusalem's strength* image by Shabtay; the *Jehovah's compassion* image by timonina; the *Judah's Savior* image by sonia; the *Anna's Communion* image by Gstudio; the *Lydia's leaven* image by Tkzgraphic; the *Nathan's window* and *Jonathan's paste* (boy) images by Nizova Tina; the paste image by Ollikeballoon; the *Noah's rainbow* image by Kiselov; the *Sarah's wool* image by Backup_studio; the *Rebekah's poetry* image by Toyotoyo; the *Elisabeth's crown* image by Olga Naidenova; the *Stephen's wood* image by The Last Word; the *Jesus's myrrh* image by C Design Studio; the *Moses's wisdom* image by Siberian Art; the *Thomas's jeopardy game* image by Yusufdemirci; and the *bushes' leaves* image by Piyathida P.

Printed and bound in the United States of America

Published by Habakkuk Educational Materials

Visit www.habakkuk.net

TEACHING KIDS ABOUT APOSTROPHE "S" IN POSSESSIVES helps students to learn that an apostrophe *s* is added to nouns and to some pronouns to show ownership. The book begins with a chart that summarizes how to form the possessive of singular nouns, of singular nouns that end with *s*, and of plurals that end with *-s* and *-es*.

After reviewing the chart at the beginning of the book, the teacher reads the words at the top and bottom of the page, leaving out the apostrophe *s* sound. Instead of saying "Aaron's bowl," for example, the teacher would say "Aaron bowl." (Students will likely note that it doesn't sound right without the apostrophe *s* sound.) Children then repeat the same words with the apostrophe *s* added—"Aaron's bowl." The apostrophe *s* shows that the bowl belongs to Aaron. Under the illustration, there is a sentence where the name with the apostrophe *s* is used in context. While this is not a storybook, the sentences on a page do relate and even rhyme. A few pages are educational in other ways besides teaching about apostrophe *s*. For instance, one page lists the order of the colors of a rainbow and includes the acronym for memorizing them. At the end of the book, you will find several reproducible worksheets that can be used for individual practice.

This book is a part of the Habakkuk Educational Materials Reading Program, designed to teach primary grade students how to read. As such, the purpose of this resource is not only to teach children about possessives but also to help them learn to recognize various names and words they will encounter in other reading materials in this program, namely *Bible History for Children and Youth (Text and Study Guide)*, *Old Testament Textbook and Study Guides for Students*, and *New Testament Textbook and Study Guides for Students*.

For more information or to contact Habakkuk Educational Materials, please visit the website below.

https://www.habakkuk.net/

Apostrophe *s*

Jo**'s** umbrella

Jo**'s** umbrella keeps her dry.

When a word does not end with *s* and you have not added an *-s* or *-es* to make it mean more than one, add an apostrophe *s* ('s) to show ownership. (Jo's umbrella, the farmer's chores)

Luca**s'**_ truck

Luca**s's** truck is red.

When a word that means one ends with *s*, you must use an apostrophe to show ownership, but it is up to you whether or not to add the *s*. (*Lucas' truck* or *Lucas's truck*)

The farmer**s'** chores

The farmers' chores are almost done.

If you have added an *-s* or *-es* to the end of a noun to make it mean more than one, insert the apostrophe after the *-s* to show ownership.

We can add an **apostrophe *s***, also called a ***possessive s***, to a person's name (as well as to other nouns and to some pronouns) to show that something belongs to the person or thing. (Josh's horse)

Aaron's bowl

Aaron's bowl of salad
will be eaten before bed.

He also wants a piece
of Alexander's bread.

Alexander's bread

April's comprehension

April's comprehension of space was helpful to some.

She told them where Jupiter's glow comes from.

Jupiter's glow

Asia's education

Asia's education will
help her to succeed.

She read Jesse's paper and
gave him good advice, indeed.

Jesse's paper

Benjamin's effort

Benjamin's effort to make better grades helped him win!

Caleb's email with the good news made him grin.

Caleb's email

Carole's advice

Carole's advice is to talk to God every day.

We can feel Christ's presence when we pray.

Christ's presence

David's 23rd Psalm

We learn that the Lord is our Shepherd in David's 23rd Psalm.

Have you heard about Adam's paradise and the apple in his palm?

Adam's paradise

Egypt's future

Egypt's future is looking bright.

Pharaoh's judgment
was not always right.

Pharaoh's judgment

Note: In ancient Egypt, whoever was the king was called Pharaoh \fā-rō\.

Eli's gratitude

Eli's gratitude is nice to see!

He's one of Abraham's beloved children, just like me.

Abraham's beloved children

Note: Abraham's children live all over the world. They include those of us who have put our faith in Christ (Galatians 3:7).

Elijah's guest

Elijah's guest is already here.

They went next door
to see Christian's gear.

Christian's gear

Elisha's guidance

Elisha's guidance helps
him to get around.

They searched for Rhoda's thread,
but it couldn't be found.

Rhoda's thread

Hannah's dough

Hannah's dough is flat for now.

It will rise like Rachel's loaves somehow.

Rachel's loaves

Haven's height

Haven's height is almost five feet.

He's as tall as Levi's spear,
which he thinks is neat.

Levi's spear

Isaac's juice

Do you see Isaac's juice in his hand?

He borrows Josiah's salt so that his soup isn't bland.

Josiah's salt

Jason's news

Jason's news made
his parents feel good.

Oklahoma's curriculum
showed their son that he could.

Oklahoma's curriculum

Jerusalem's strength

Jerusalem's strength comes
from God, as we know.

We prayed for Jehovah's compassion
at the Wailing Wall not long ago.

Jehovah's compassion

Note: Jerusalem is the capital of Israel. Jehovah is another name for God. The bottom image shows Jewish men praying at the Wailing Wall (also called the Western Wall) in the Old City of Jerusalem.

Judah's Savior

Judah's Savior is
the Son of God.

He went to Anna's
Communion and was awed.

Anna's Communion

Lydia's leaven

Lydia's leaven causes her cake to rise.

This cake for Michael's baptism is just the right size.

Michael's baptism

Nathan's window

How did Nathan's window break?

Trying to fix it with Jonathan's paste would be a mistake.

Jonathan's paste

Noah's rainbow

The colors of Noah's rainbow
are in the correct order, it's true.

Which colors are in Sarah's
wool scarf besides blue?

Sarah's wool

Note: The acronym Roy G. Biv can help you to remember that the order of the colors of a rainbow are red, orange, yellow, green, blue, indigo, and violet.

Rebekah's poetry

Rebekah's poetry is
about a lovely queen.

Elisabeth's crown is
something to be seen!

Elisabeth's crown

Stephen's wood

Stephen's wood is in a pile.

When he saw Jacob's locust, it made him smile.

Jacob's locust

St. Joseph's priest

St. Joseph's priest said to donate blood this week.

Simon's blood group is O+, and that's what they seek.

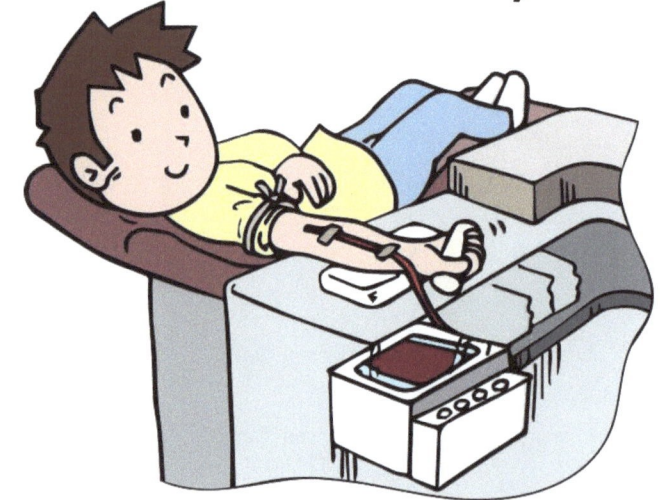

Simon's blood group

Jesus's myrrh

Jesus' myrrh

Jesus's myrrh was a gift from the Wise Men.

Jesus' myrrh was a gift from the Wise Men.

Note: When a noun already ends with *s* (as in *Jesus*), you can still use an apostrophe *s* to show possession (Jesus**'s**), or you could show possession by inserting the apostrophe without the *s* (Jesus**'**).

Moses's wisdom

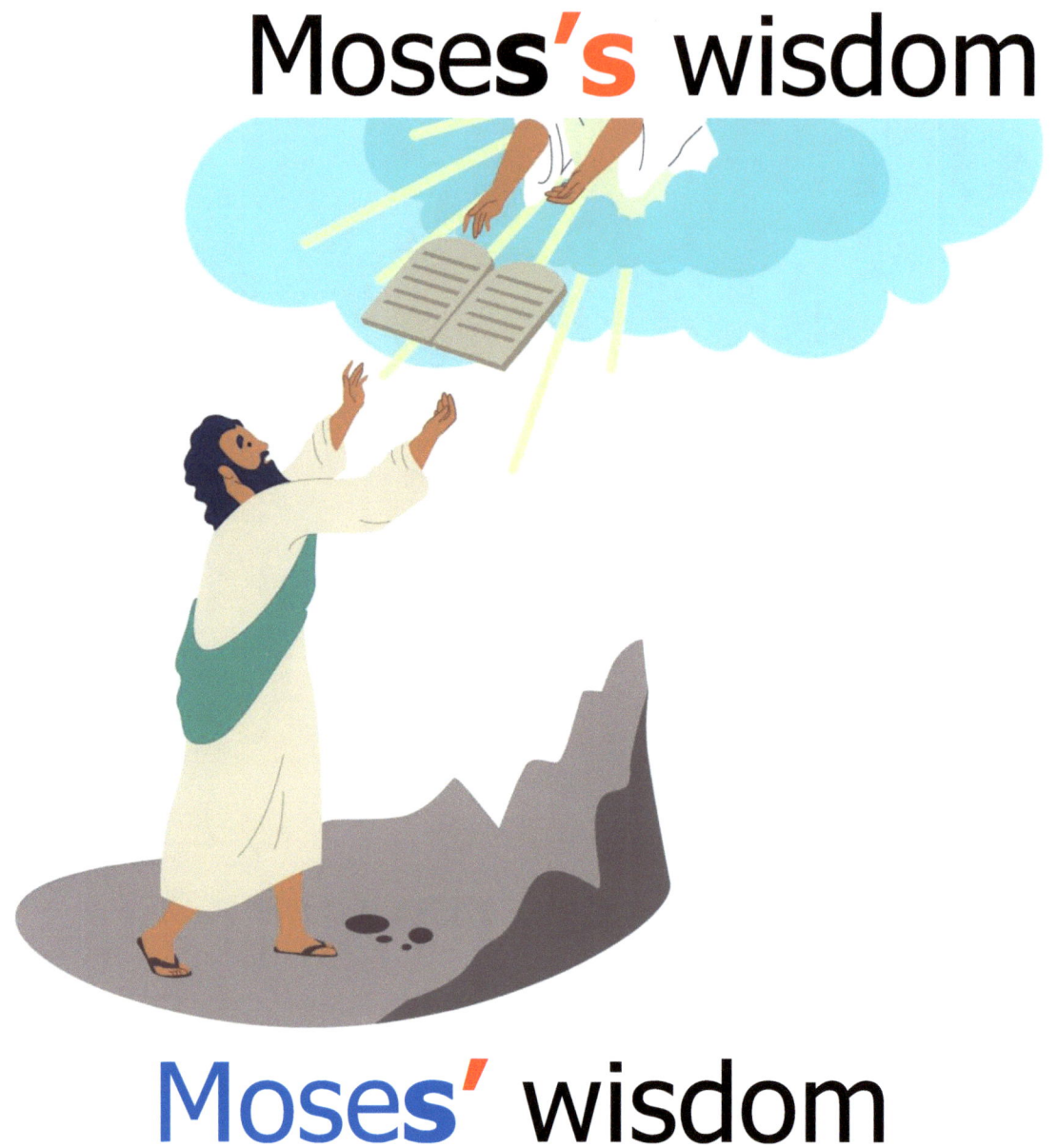

Moses' wisdom

Moses's wisdom was given to him by God.

Moses' wisdom was given to him by God.

Note: When a noun already ends with *s* (as in *Moses*), you can still use an apostrophe *s* to show possession (Moses**'s**), or you could show possession by inserting the apostrophe without the *s* (Moses**'**).

Thomas's Jeopardy game

Thomas' Jeopardy game

Thomas's Jeopardy game is wrapped.

Thomas' Jeopardy game is wrapped.

_____

Note: When a noun already ends with *s* (as in *Thomas*), you can still use an apostrophe *s* to show possession (Thomas's), or you could show possession by inserting the apostrophe without the *s* (Thomas').

The farmers' chores

The farmers' chores are almost done.

The bushes' leaves need
to be watered a ton.

The bushes' leaves

Note: If you have added an -s or -es to the end of a noun to make it mean more than one, insert the apostrophe after the -s to show ownership.

Possessive *s*

Directions: Insert an apostrophe or an apostrophe *s* in the first space to show ownership. In the second space, add an -*s* to the noun to make it mean more than one. (e.g., *Eli's cars*)

Louis__ friend__

Mandi__ bracelet__

Kingston__ toy__

The girl__ teacher__

The girls__ teacher__

Directions: Read the sentences and ask yourself if *farmer* makes sense in the context of the sentence without an apostrophe *s*. If the answer is no, insert an apostrophe *s* ('**s**) in the space provided.

1. The **farmer**___ has a red barn.

2. The **farmer**___ barn is red.

Possessive *s*

Directions: Insert an apostrophe or an apostrophe *s* in the first space to show ownership. In the second space, add an -*s* to the noun to make it mean more than one. (e.g., *Eli's cars*)

Beau___ picture___

Emily___ pet___

Charles___ book___

The students___ classroom___

The student___ classroom___

Directions: Read the sentences and ask yourself if *father* makes sense in the context of the sentence without an apostrophe *s*. If the answer is no, insert an apostrophe *s* (**'s**) in the space provided.

1. My **father**___ drives a big truck.

2. My **father**___ truck is big.

Possessive *s*

Directions: Insert an apostrophe or an apostrophe *s* in the first space to show ownership. In the second space, add an -*s* to the noun to make it mean more than one. (e.g., *Eli's cars*)

Grace___ doll___

Curtis___ pencil___

Hunter___ cousin___

The boy___ game___

The boys___ game___

Directions: Read the sentences and ask yourself if *sister* makes sense in the context of the sentence without an apostrophe *s*. If the answer is no, insert an apostrophe *s* (**'s**) in the space provided.

1. My **sister**___ got a new phone.

2. My **sister**___ phone is new.

Possessive *s*

Directions: Insert an apostrophe or an apostrophe *s* in the first space to show ownership. In the second space, add an -*s* to the noun to make it mean more than one. (e.g., *Eli's cars*)

Louis**'s** friend**s**   or   Louis**'** friend**s**

Mandi**'s** bracelet**s**

Kingston**'s** toy**s**

The girl**'s** teacher**s**

The girls**'** teacher**s**

Directions: Read the sentences and ask yourself if *farmer* makes sense in the context of the sentence without an apostrophe *s*. If the answer is no, insert an apostrophe *s* (**'s**) in the space provided.

1. The **farmer**___ has a red barn.

2. The **farmer's** barn is red.

Possessive *s*

Directions: Insert an apostrophe or an apostrophe *s* in the first space to show ownership. In the second space, add an -*s* to the noun to make it mean more than one. (e.g., *Eli's cars*)

Beau**'s** picture**s**

Emily**'s** pet**s**

Charles**'s** book**s**   or   Charles**'** book**s**

The students**'** classroom**s**

The student**'s** classroom**s**

Directions: Read the sentences and ask yourself if *father* makes sense in the context of the sentence without an apostrophe *s*. If the answer is no, insert an apostrophe *s* (**'s**) in the space provided.

1. My **father**___ drives a big truck.

2. My **father's** truck is big.

Possessive *s*

Directions: Insert an apostrophe or an apostrophe *s* in the first space to show ownership. In the second space, add an -*s* to the noun to make it mean more than one. (e.g., *Eli's cars*)

Grace**'s** doll**s**

Curtis**'s** pencil**s**   or   Curtis**'** pencil**s**

Hunter**'s** cousin**s**

The boy**'s** game**s**

The boys**'** game**s**

Directions: Read the sentences and ask yourself if *sister* makes sense in the context of the sentence without an apostrophe *s*. If the answer is no, insert an apostrophe *s* (**'s**) in the space provided.

1. My **sister's** phone is new.

2. My **sister**___ got a new phone.

www.ingramcontent.com/pod-product-compliance
Lightning Source LLC
Chambersburg PA
CBHW041539040426
42446CB00002B/151